This book highlights the sights and delights of London. It picks out the premier not-to-be-missed places to visit together with a selection of the most interesting historic, cultural or popular facets of London life that can be enjoyed at leisure.

Places are grouped in sections according to location or subject. A map at the beginning of each section pinpoints the places mentioned in the text to make visiting them easier, either by foot or by public transport.

For details of opening times and nearest underground stations, please refer to "Essential Information" on pages 62-63.

This guidebook is a companion to Over London, which gives an equally fascinating but wholly different pictorial view of London - from the air.

The City

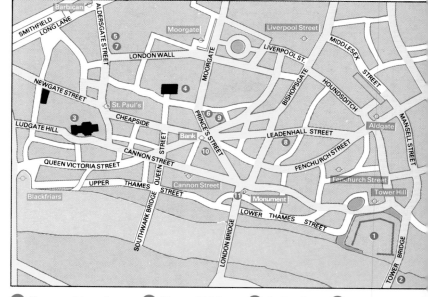

1 Tower of London **2** Tower Bridge **3** St Paul's **4** Guildhall
5 Barbican Centre **6** Bank of England **7** Museum of London **8** Lloyd's
9 Stock Exchange **10** Mansion House **11** Monument

The story of London begins, as it did centuries ago, in the 'square mile' called the City. Here, within its boundaries, can be found landmarks to London's fortunes through the ages.

The Romans laid the first foundations of London with a permanent fortified and walled settlement in the area which rapidly became a thriving trading centre.

The Norman invasion a thousand years later gave the City a fortress which has symbolised military might and power ever since: **The Tower of London** (*photographs 1-7*). It has been a citadel, royal palace, seat of government and also the scene of some of the bloodiest events in English history. Kings, queens, princes and people of the highest rank have shared the same fate within its walls as spies, plotters and traitors. The Tower of

London is where they were tortured, beheaded, murdered or imprisoned.

It is also the nation's treasure house, containing the Crown Jewels.

William the Conqueror planned his massive fortress to protect the city, subdue and overawe its citizens and guard the approach to London by river from its strategic position at the City's eastern boundary.

The White Tower (*photograph page 1*), dating from 1078, has walls 11-15 feet thick and was built of white Caen stone from Normandy. It contains a spectacular collection of arms and armour (*photographs page 6*). The oldest church in London, the Chapel of St John dating from 1080, lies within the White Tower's walls.

From this central dominant Norman keep, the Tower of London grew over 400 years. Ringed by two protective walls both strung with numerous towers, these in turn are surrounded and defended by a moat - dry now - and drawbridges. Yet this formidable fortress has never been seriously put to the test in its 900 year history.

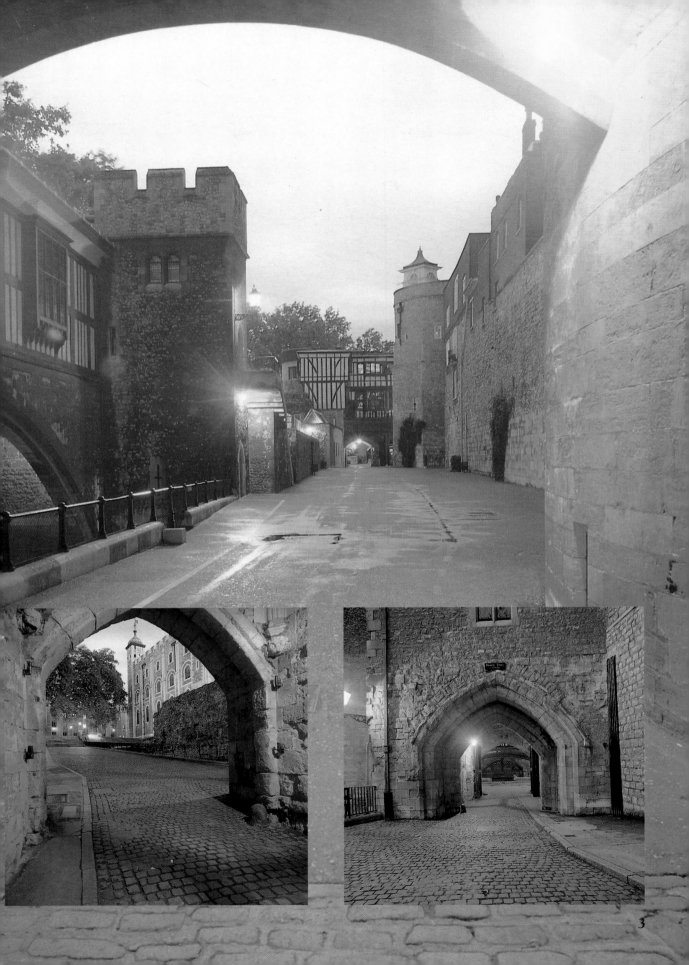

Traitor's Gate, with an arch 60 feet wide, was the entrance to The Tower for those accused of plotting against the state. It gave direct entry to The Tower by boat or barge from the River Thames, whose waters filled the moat.

The Bloody Tower is where the 'Little Princes' - Edward V and his brother Richard - were believed to have been smothered in 1483.

The Tower has been associated with sensational events throughout its history. One king's exploits in particular have left a notorious mark. King Henry VIII was married in The Tower to Catherine of Aragon in 1509. Her successor, Anne Boleyn, rode to her coronation from The Tower and was beheaded in the same place in 1536. A similar fate befell Henry's fifth queen, Catherine Howard, in 1542. The Tower's prisoners have included King David II of Scotland in the 14th century, Princess (later Queen) Elizabeth in the 16th century, Guy Fawkes and his fellow conspirators who plotted to blow up the Houses of Parliament in the 17th century, and Rudolph Hess, Hitler's deputy, in the 20th century.

Tower Green is where many of royal and noble birth met their death. Nearby is the Chapel Royal of St Peter ad Vincula (St Peter in Chains) where many victims are buried (*photograph page 7*).

Ravens can always be seen on Tower Green. Their disappearance is said to herald the fall of the British Empire and the White Tower, so their wings are clipped to confine them. A Raven Master feeds and protects them.

As well as being home to the gory relics of English history, The Tower also houses its glory. The Crown Jewels (*photograph page 7*) are permanently on display in a specially built modern vault.

The oldest crown in the royal regalia is St Edward's, made for the coronation of King Charles II in 1661 and still used for the coronation ceremony. The Imperial State Crown, made for Queen Victoria's coronation in 1838, is set with 3,000 diamonds and other precious stones, including the ruby given to the Black Prince in 1367 and worn by King Henry V at the battle of Agincourt in 1415. At the brow of the crown is one of the Stars of Africa diamonds cut from the Cullinan, the largest diamond ever found, which weighed one and a half pounds uncut. The Crown of Queen Elizabeth made in 1937 is set with the Koh-i-noor or 'Mountain of Light' diamond whose legendary history goes back five thousand years.

Ceremonial is still part of the daily life within The Tower. Each night the Chief Warder locks the gates and presents the keys to the Resident Governor - a ritual that has taken place for 700 years. Yeoman warders who assist today's visitors to The Tower still wear the distinctive colourful uniform dating from Tudor times. (*photograph page 2*).

An opening in the wall by Traitor's Gate leads to Tower Wharf where cannon gun salutes are fired to mark significant royal events and

anniversaries. Tower Wharf offers a strategic view of London's most famous bridge. A miracle of hydraulic engineering **Tower Bridge** (*front cover, photograph page 8*) raises its 1,000 ton drawbridges as if in salute to allow tall ships to pass between its twin Gothic-style towers. Rising from the river bed, the towers house the original machinery which lifts the roadway in one and a half minutes. Started

in 1886 and finished in 1894 at a cost of £800,000, Tower Bridge has been raised over half a million times since it was built. The towers are connected at the top by a walkway 142 feet above the water level. Designers of the bridge were Sir Horace Jones, who died as work began, and Sir John Wolfe Barry.

St Paul's Cathedral - the spiritual centre of the City - rose out of the devastation of the Great Fire of London of 1666 which razed two thirds of London to ashes in four days. It was the fifth cathedral to be built on the site and the present building, completed in 1710, has remained largely unaltered to this day.

St Paul's (*phogographs pages 9-12*) has been the setting for solemn and significant occasions in the nation's history, from the funeral of Sir Winston Churchill to the wedding of the Prince and Princess of Wales.

King Charles II authorised the new cathedral building in 1673 and a higher tax on coal entering the Port of London was levied to pay for it. The King knighted the chosen architect Sir Christopher Wren, before building started as a sign of his confidence. After the old cathedral had been cleared from the site, Sir Christopher called for a stone to mark out the foundations of

the new. A workman chose one at random from a heap of rubble. It was part of a broken tombstone carved with the word RESURGAM (I shall rise again). From the foundations rose the magnificent Renaissance building seen today.

Built of Portland stone, the cathedral's main west front portico, carved with a sculpture of the conversion of St Paul, is flanked by two towers (*photograph page 12*). The north tower contains a peal of twelve bells and the south houses a clock and Great Paul, the largest bell in England, weighing over 16 tons.

The Dome, the second larges in the world after St Peter's in Rome, rises 365 feet into the air and supports a lantern and cross weighing around 700 tons.

The altar is a modern monument to those who died in the two World Wars (*photograph page 10*). The

fine woodcarving on the choir stalls is the work of Grinling Gibbons, whose craftsmanship can also be seen at Windsor Castle and Hampton Court.

Steps lead to the Dome's Whispering Gallery (a word whispered into the wall will be clearly heard on the other side). This is the best vantage point to view Sir James Thornhill's decoration of the Dome depicting the life of St Paul. More steps lead up to the Stone and Golden Galleries. A ball and cross surmount the top.

St Paul's contains monuments to the nation's heroes, including Admiral Nelson (*photograph page 12*) and the Duke of Wellington; statesmen, writers and artists. But the simplest and humblest epitaph is to St Paul's architect, Sir Christopher Wren. Translated from Latin it says: "Reader, if you seek a

monument, look about you."

The City of London today is the financial powerhouse of London. Bankers, brokers, buyers and traders conduct their daily business within its boundaries. Here, the ancient halls of the medieval craft guilds shelter in the shadow of modern steel and glass office blocks like the controversial **Lloyd's** building (*photograph page 13*) and the **Stock Exchange.**

The Bank of England (*photograph page 14*) in Threadneedle Street is the national bank. Its vaults hold the country's gold reserves. The Bank is popularly known as the 'Old Lady of Threadneedle Street' - a reference to the sculpture of Britannia over the main entrance.

The City has its own Lord Mayor, its own government and its own police force. Even the sovereign has to stop at the City's frontiers until

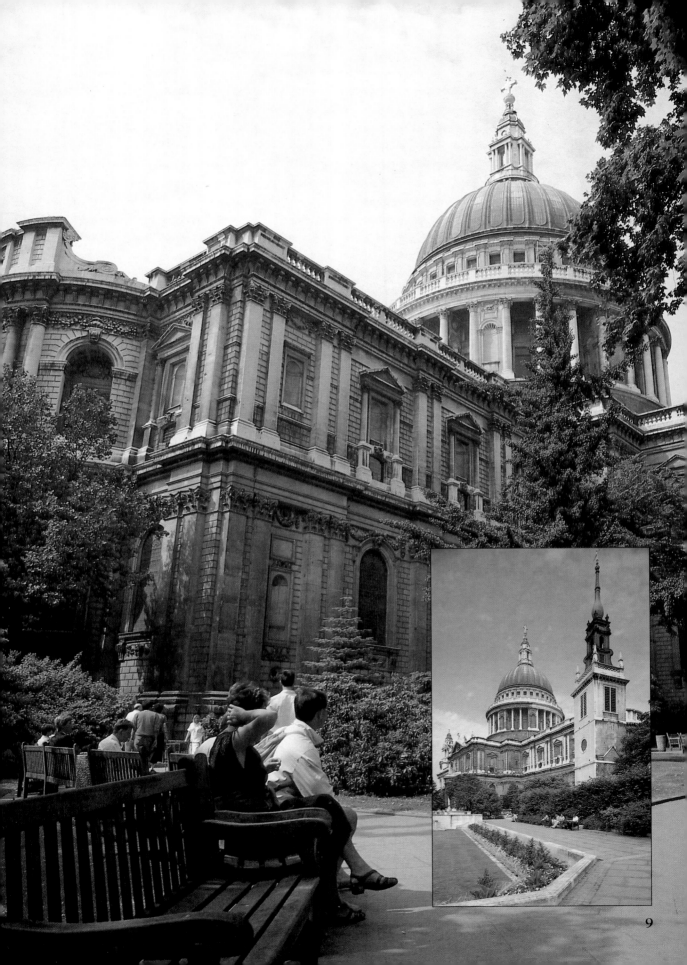

Photograph above left is of the Tijou Gates.

Top right shows part of the brass eagle lectern with organ in the background. The carvings on the organ are by Grinling Gibbons.

Above: This is the view of the inside of the dome and the Whispering Gallery. The inner dome is decorated with frescos painted by James Thornhill.

Left: The American Memorial Chapel and the Roll of Honour. This roll lists the 28,000 members of the American forces based in Britain, who lost their lives during the Second World War. It was presented to St. Paul's in 1951 by General Eisenhower. The rebuilding of the Chapel was completed in 1958.

Lloyds of London.

Left: St. Paul's Cathedral

13

the Lord Mayor allows admittance.
The Guildhall, dating from the
15th century, is where the Lord
Mayor, Aldermen and City fathers
conduct the City's affairs.
Important banquets and ceremonial
occasions are held there. **The
Mansion House,** built in 1735, is
the official home of the Lord Mayor,
who holds office for a year.

The Monument, *(photograph page
14)* a 202 feet high stone column,
commemorates the Great Fire of
London of 1666 which broke out in
a baker's shop in Pudding Lane, 202
feet away from the column's plinth.

Designed by Sir Christopher Wren,
it symbolises the City's ability to
restore itself from disaster.

From a bombsite, the **Barbican
Centre** has developed into a vast 60-
acre commercial, residential and
leisure complex. The Centre includes
a concert hall, exhibition gallery,
cinema, restaurants, bars, gardens and
theatre (the London home of the
Royal Shakespeare Company).

The Museum of London depicts
London's history from prehistory to
the present day, with many
archaeological finds on display.

Westminster

Concentrated within a half-mile square of Westminster are the centres of power in British life:

. Civil power is represented by parliament and government, based in the **Houses of Commons and Lords** and in **Whitehall;**

. Spiritual power is focused in Westminster's historic **Abbey** and **Cathedral.**

For 900 years, nearly every king or queen of England has been crowned in Westminster Abbey (*photograph page 16*).

The Abbey was refounded in the 11th century by a king - Edward the Confessor - and the strong royal link and special royal status have been maintained over the centuries. Many English monarchs are buried here.

The site had been used as a place of worship for centuries earlier. Its name refers to its position to the west of the City of London - 'west monastery' or Westminster. Minster means 'large church'.

The magnificent Gothic building seen today largely dates from the 13th and 14th centuries, although the Chapel of the Pyx and the Undercroft (now the Abbey museum) are 11th century.

The Abbey Museum features wooden or wax funerary effigies of monarchs and treasures including Henry V's shield and helmet from the battle field of Agincourt.

Monuments to those who were born to high rank and those who achieved glory line the walls of the Abbey.

St Edward the Confessor's chapel, the most sacred part of the Abbey, is the burial place of kings. But a simple black marble slab in the nave pays tribute to those unknown and unsung heroes who also served their country - the tomb of the unknown warrior. Beside it is a green marble slab to the memory of Sir Winston Churchill.

The Sanctuary, within the altar rails, is the setting of coronations. Behind the 15th century carved stone screen, which forms the back of the high altar, stands the oak Coronation Chair (*photograph page 18*) Underneath it is the famous

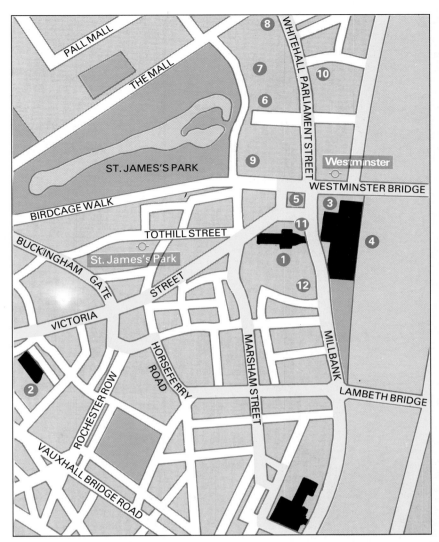

1 **Westminster Abbey** 2 **Westminster Cathedral** 3 **Big Ben**
4 **Houses of Parliament** 5 **Parliament Square** 6 **Downing Street**
7 **Horse Guards** 8 **Whitehall** 9 **Cabinet War Rooms**
10 **Banqueting House** 11 **St. Margarets Church** 12 **Jewel Tower**

Stone of Scone, a block of sandstone used as the coronation seat of the kings of Scotland from the 8th century. It was seized by King Edward I in 1297 as a sign of the subjugation of Scotland to the English crown.

Henry VII's chapel is notable for the delicate and intricate fan vaulting of its roof. The Abbey nave vaulting is the highest of any church in England at 103 feet.

The 16 Waterford crystal chandeliers which hang in the Abbey were a gift to mark in 1965 the 900th anniversary of its consecration.

Opening off the east walk of the cloisters is the Chapter House, an octagonal chamber 60 feet across dating from the 13th century. Called 'the cradle of all free parliaments' it was the meeting place for Parliament from the 14th to the 16th centuries.

In the Chamber of Pyx, part of Edward the Confessor's church, was stored the 'pyx' or chest containing the trial plates of gold and silver used as the standards of quality for coins of the realm.

The Abbey precincts, which include Dean's Yard on the site of the Abbey gardens, are a quiet and timeless sanctuary.

Westminster Abbey towers over **St Margaret's,** the parish church of the House of Commons. Founded in the 11th or 12th century, it has been a fashionable place for weddings over the centuries. Diarist Samuel Pepys was married here in 1655, the poet John Milton a year later and Winston Churchill in 1908.

Westminster Cathedral (*photograph page 19*) is the leading Roman Catholic church in England. Designed by John Francis Bentley and built around the turn of the century in Byzantine style, its red brick (twelve and a half million of them) and white Portland stone give its exterior a striking striped

appearance. This is highlighted by the campanile, 273 feet high, which stands out like a beacon over the surrounding area. The cross, 11 feet high, that tops the campanile contains a relic of the True Cross.

The cathedral is 342 feet long, 117 feet to the top of the domes and the nave is the widest in England at

60 feet across, giving the interior a feeling of massive magnificence. While the bare walls and vaults were designed to be covered with mosaics and marble, the intended effect can be seen in the cathedral's chapels, notably the elaborately decorated Lady Chapel. Eric Gill's relief depicting Stations of the Cross is considered one of the cathedral's treasures.

Sir Winston Churchill's statue *(photograph page 22)* is among those of famous statesmen and former prime ministers in **Parliament Square.** A patch of green uniting the House of Commons on one side, Westminster Abbey on another and Whitehall, Parliament Square was laid out by Sir Charles Barry, architect of the **Houses of Parliament** *(photographs pages 20-21).*

The Houses of Parliament form an elaborate Gothic-style carved stone group of buildings on the banks of the River Thames. Here laws governing British life are formulated, debated and passed. Begun in 1840, after a disastrous fire destroyed the previous building, the Houses of Parliament cover eight acres and include 100 staircases, eleven courtyards, more than 1,000 apartments and two miles of passages. Its official title is New Palace of Westminster, as a royal palace has existed on the site since the 11th century.

One of the best known landmarks in the world is the 320 feet high clock tower, popularly known as Big Ben *(photograph back cover).* This is actually the name of the thirteen and a half ton bell that strikes the hours. The clock's four dials are each 23 feet across and the hands over 14 feet long. A light in the tower at night shows whether the House of Commons is sitting. At the opposite corner of the building rises the Victoria Tower, the largest and tallest square tower in the world. Through its archway the monarch enters for the State Opening of Parliament each November.

In 1605, Guy Fawkes and fellow Roman Catholic conspirators were discovered in the cellars ready to blow up King James I together with the Lords and Commons as they assembled for the opening of Parliament on 5 November. The vaults are still searched by Yeomen of the Guard each year before the State Opening of a new Parliamentary session.

The British people are represented in the House of Commons by 650 Members of Parliament. The House of Lords comprises peers of the realm - dukes, earls, countesses, marquises, viscounts, barons and baronesses - and archbishops and bishops. Their Lordships' chamber *(photograph page 23)* is a richly carved hall with a dais for the monarch's ornate throne. In front of the throne is the Woolsack, a seat stuffed with the wool from

Britain and the Commonwealth which has traditionally stood in the House since the time of Edward III in the 14th century. This is the seat of the Lord Chancellor when the House is sitting.

The House of Commons, completely destroyed in an air-raid in 1941, is simpler in style. The green leather parallel rows of benches that face towards the well of the chamber offer seating for only two thirds of the 650 elected members at any one time. The mace (a symbol of authority) is placed on a table in the centre of the chamber at the start of each day's proceedings. Each daily sitting is presided over by the Speaker.

Westminster Hall (*photograph page 22*), the great hall of the royal palace, is the only remaining medieval part of the complex apart from St Stephen's Crypt and the Jewel Tower. King Charles I stood trial at Westminster Hall after he lost the Civil War and was sentenced to die. His adversary, Oliver Cromwell, who established supremacy of Parliament over the monarchy and made England a republic for 11 years, is commemorated by a statue erected in front of Westminster Hall.

Whitehall is named after a royal palace which existed on the site. It burned down in 1698 when one of King William's Dutch laundry maids hung some clothes to dry too close to a charcoal fire. The Palace was razed to the ground by the next day. The only remaining part is the Banqueting House, a masterpiece of classical architecture by Inigo Jones which was built in the 17th century. Its ceilings were painted by Rubens.

The Horse Guards, whose entrance is guarded by two mounted troopers of the Household Cavalry, was built on the site of the guardhouse for the old palace of Whitehall. The troopers are at their posts daily from 10 am to 4 pm. At 11 am (10 am on Sundays) the colourful ceremony of Changing the Guard is performed (*photograph page 23*).

Government offices line both sides of Whitehall. **The Cenotaph**

Top: Westminster Cathedral.

Bottom: St. Margaret's & Westminster Abbey.

Left: Big Ben.
Top: Aerial view of the Houses of Parliament
Bottom: Parliament Square.

(*photograph page 22*), a memorial to those who died in 20th century wars, forms an island in the centre of the broad road. Each year on Remembrance Sunday (in November) a two minute silence is observed during a service attended by the Queen and royal family, statemen and representatives of the armed forces and Commonwealth.

The official home of the Prime Minister, number **10 Downing Street,** leads off Whitehall. During rebuilding work behind its Georgian facade in the 1960s were found remains of Roman pottery, a Saxon hall and the Tudor palace of Whitehall. Downing Street was named after George Downing, a diplomat, spy and property developer. He was taken as a child to Massachusetts in America but returned home when Oliver Cromwell seized power. After becoming

21

Cromwell's chief spy on the Continent, he switched sides to spy for King Charles I and was rewarded with a knighthood and a crown lease on the parcel of land. He developed the site which subsequently became home to successive British Prime Ministers from 1735 onward.

Sixty rooms lie behind the narrow front. The Cabinet Room is on the ground floor and State Rooms on the first where official receptions and banquets are held. A door and passageway lead from number 10 to number 11 next door - the official residence of the Chancellor of the Exchequer.

The underground **Cabinet War Rooms** in King Charles Street now show visitors where the cabinet, led by Churchill, met in the 1940s when London was under attack during World War II.

Top: Changing the Guards at Whitehall.

Right: The House of Lords.

Trafalgar Square & The Royal Palaces

From his perch 167 feet above **Trafalgar Square** (*photograph page 26*), Admiral Lord Nelson surveys the memorial to his great naval victory in 1805. Laid out in 1840 by Sir Charles Barry, who designed the Houses of Parliament, Trafalgar Square is a popular venue for political demonstrations - and pigeons.

The Admiral's statue, 17 feet high and carved in granite, looks towards the Houses of Parliament at the end of Whitehall. Four panels at the foot of the famous column cast from captured cannons depict the Battles of St Vincent and the Nile, the Bombardment of Copenhagen and the death of Nelson. Four magnificent bronze lions, each 20 feet long and 11 feet high, stand guard. The fountains in the square were remodelled in 1939 to the designs of Sir Edwin Lutyens. Every Christmas, a fir tree is set up in Trafalgar Square (*photograph page 28*), a gift from the people of Norway in thanks for the hospitality shown by the British nation to their Royal Family during World War II.

The National Gallery's classical columns provide the backdrop for the north side of the square. Containing one of the richest and most extensive collections of art in the world, the National Gallery was built on the site of a royal stables. Behind the National Gallery is the National Portrait Gallery, a pictorial hall of fame whose treasures include a painting of Queen Elizabeth I after the triumphant defeat of the Spanish Armada.

St Martin-in-the-Fields (*photograph page 28*), a classical masterpiece by James Gibbs dating from 1721, stands at the square's north-east corner. A church has existed on the site since the 12th century. St Martin is the patron saint of beggars.

South Africa House bounds the east side of the square; Canada House the west.

Admiralty Arch (*photographs pages 28-29*) was erected in 1910 as one of the national memorials to Queen Victoria. It leads to **The Mall**, the

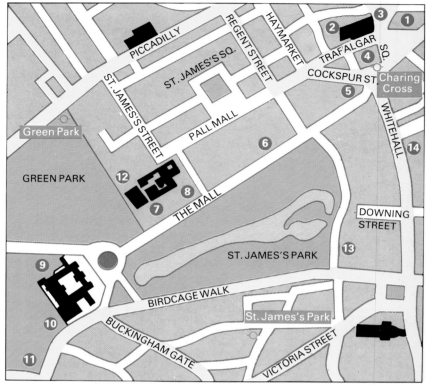

1. St. Martin in the Fields   2. National Gallery   3. Portrait Gallery
4. Nelson's Column   5. Admiralty Arch   6. The Mall   7. Clarence House
8. St. James's Palace   9. Buckingham Palace   10. Queen's Gallery
11. Royal Mews   12. Lancaster House   13. Cabinet War Rooms
14. Banqueting House

route of royal and state processions whose name derives from the game of 'paille-maille', similar to croquet, that was popularly played here during the 17th century.

The area of **St James's** is named after a hospital for lepers, dedicated to St James in the 13th century. At St James Palace (*photograph page 29*), King Charles I spent his last night alive before his walk across St James's Park to Whitehall, where he was executed.

When the monarchy was restored

Aerial view of Buckingham Palace and St. James's.

Painting of Horatio Nelson by Sir William Beechey at the National Portrait Gallery.

The Virgin and Child with St. Anne and St. John the Baptist by Leonardo da Vinci from the National Gallery.

in 1660, King Charles II made the palace at St James's his principal home and it has been a favourite of later monarchs over the centuries. It is to the Court of St James that all foreign ambassadors still present their credentials. St James's Palace is now the official office of the Lord Chamberlain's department.

Clarence House, at the south-west front of St James's Palace, was added in 1825 and is the London home of Her Majesty Queen Elizabeth the Queen Mother. Across the stable yard from St James's Palace is Lancaster House, a richly decorated setting for great state occasions and banquets.

At the head of The Mall is the **Queen Victoria Memorial.** The statue of the seated monarch lies in the shadow of the best-known palace in the world: **Buckingham Palace** (*photograph page 29*).

Built in 1703 for the Duke of Buckingham, it was bought sixty years later by King George III for £28,000. His extravagant but stylish son, King George IV commissioned John Nash,

the court architect, to remodel it in 1824. George IV's sucessor, Queen Victoria, made it the permanent home of the court in 1837, but by 1846 the palace was too small for her growing family so an east wing was added in 1847. The present stern but dignified classical front, 390 feet long and built of Portland stone, was reconstructed in 1913. The first floor balcony is the scene of formal appearances of the royal family on important occasions. Below it in the forecourt, the colourful ceremony of Changing the Guard takes place (*photograph page 33*).

The Royal Family occupies the north wing of the palace and the Royal Standard is flown when the Queen is in residence.

The interior of the palace is open to the public, during the months of August and September, for a rare glimpse of the splendours inside. The State Rooms are used to receive visiting heads of state and for investiture ceremonies where the Queen and other members of the royal family bestow titles, honours and awards for outstanding service.

The west front of the palace overlooks a private 40-acre expanse of lawns and lake.

The former private chapel of Buckingham Palace which was bombed in 1940 and rebuilt in the 1960s houses the **Queen's Gallery.** Some of the finest art treasures of the royal collection can now be viewed by the public. **The Royal Mews** (*photograph page 29*), where the Queen's horses are stabled, is also open to the public. Built by John Nash in 1826, the Royal Mews

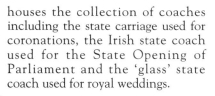

houses the collection of coaches including the state carriage used for coronations, the Irish state coach used for the State Opening of Parliament and the 'glass' state coach used for royal weddings.

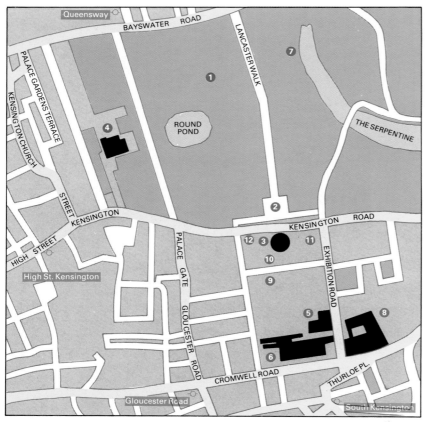

1 Kensington Gardens   **2** Albert Memorial   **3** Royal Albert Hall

4 Kensington Palace   **5** Science Museum   **6** Natural History Museum

7 Statue of Peter Pan   **8** Victoria & Albert Museum

9 Royal College of Music   **10** Imperial College

11 Royal Geographical Society   **12** Royal College of Art

Kensington

Kensington is one of London's royal boroughs. The Prince and Princess of Wales are among the many members of the royal family who continue a royal tradition by making it their London base.

Kensington Palace (*photograph page 31*) was formerly the home of the Earl of Nottingham. King William III, an asthmatic who found the air of Whitehall disagreeable and crowds objectionable, bought the house in 1689 for £18,000 and employed Sir Christopher Wren, architect of St Paul's, to rebuild it. The south wing of the red brick Palace is the notable surviving part of Wren's work. Later monarchs ordered subsequent improvements and alterations.

The State Apartments were restored and opened to the public in 1975.

King William's Gallery, designed by Wren, features fine wood-carving, probably by the master-carver Grinling Gibbons, and a selection of paintings from the Queen's private collection. Mementos of Queen Victoria, who was born and lived at Kensington Palace as a princess, include her toys and dolls' house. The Cupola room, where Princess Victoria was christened, is one of the most extravagantly decorated State Rooms.

The private part of the Palace is now a select series of apartments for the Princess of Wales, Princess Margaret and other royal relatives.

Kensington Gardens, once the private grounds of the Palace, is now a public park, separated from Hyde Park by the Serpentine lake. Features include the Orangery, now containing statuary, a sunken garden and the statue of Peter Pan (*photograph page 30*), hero of Sir James Barrie's fairy story. It was erected in 1912, at night, to surprise the local children. In the children's playground stands the Elfin Oak, an old stump carved with figures of fairies, elves and animals.

The Albert Memorial (*photograph page 32*) is within Kensington Gardens. The elaborate memorial to Prince Albert, Consort to Queen Victoria, was erected between 1863-76. The Prince in gilt-bronze is depicted under an ornate canopy, a copy of the catalogue of the Great Exhibition on his lap. He inspired the idea of the Great Exhibition in 1851 as a showcase of British artistic and engineering expertise and craftsmanship. The exhibition also raised money to build Kensington's museums nearby.

The Albert Memorial is opposite the **Royal Albert Hall** (*photograph page 32*), an oval amphitheatre covered by a glass dome - the home of good music from the classical Promenade concerts to pop.

Completed in 1871 to the designs of Captain Francis Fowke, it measures 273 feet across, 155 feet high and is capable of accommodating audiences of up to 8,000 people. The Hall's famous organ, with nearly 10,000 pipes, is one of the mightiest in the world.

The Victoria and Albert Museum is a national collection of fine and applied art. Over its main entrance in Cromwell Road are statues of Queen Victoria and Prince Albert. The museum has around seven miles of galleries and exhibits ranging from the 16th century Great Bed of Ware to the Canning Jewel, a merman forged in precious gold and jewels and brought from India by Lord Canning after the Mutiny of 1857-59. The museum is a vast treasure house of arts and crafts culled from all periods and cultures.

The Science Museum's emphasis on working models which visitors can explore and handle brings science to life. It shows scientific discoveries and the evolution of technology to the present day.

The Natural History Museum (*photograph page 32*) covers botany, entomology, minerology, palaeontology and zoology, with stuffed exhibits ranging from dinosaurs to minute preserved insects from all over the world.

Kensington Palace Gardens.

Legal, Regal & Ceremonial London

The pomp, pageantry and solemn ceremony of important state and legal events in London is a vivid living link with the past. London may have changed over the centuries, but its dignified, traditional customs have not.

Many of Britain's rich treasury of regular ceremonials are centred around the monarchy. **Trooping the Colour** (*photographs pages 34-35*), held early in June to celebrate the Queen's official birthday, is an elaborate, colourful event carried out by the sovereign's personal troops on Horse Guards Parade.

The ceremony stemmed from the need of soldiers to recognise the Colours of their regiment in battle. The parade is complex and precise and all regiments of the Household Division take part, but only one

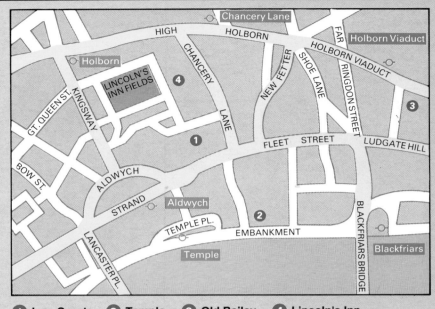

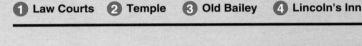
1 Law Courts   **2** Temple   **3** Old Bailey   **4** Lincoln's Inn

Colour is trooped each year. After inspecting her troops, the sovereign watches a display of marching to the tune of massed bands. The highlight of the ceremony is the solemn moment when the Colour is trooped by being carried along the motionless ranks of guardsmen. The Royal Family later appear on the balcony of Buckingham Palace to acknowledge a fly-past of the Royal Air Force.

The Guards have been carrying out their duty of guarding the

Trooping the Colour.

Below: The State Opening of Parliament.

sovereign since 1660. The ceremony of **Changing the Guard** (*photograph page 33*) which lasts about half an hour, is one of the

most popular sights for tourists. It takes place at Buckingham Palace at 11.30 daily (on alternate days mid-August to March) and at 11 am Monday to Saturday (or daily if the Queen is in residence there) at Windsor Castle. The mounted Guard of Household Cavalry is ceremonially changed at Whitehall at 11 am daily (10 am on Sunday).

The ceremonial and pageantry of a State Visit serves two purposes: to welcome important guests from abroad and to impress them with symbols of the nation's power and prestige. As part of the welcoming reception, a carriage procession along the traditional State Drive to the royal palace - either Buckingham Palace or Windsor Castle - is escorted by a Sovereign's Escort. Flags are hung along the route.

Royal Salutes are fired throughout the year at Hyde Park and the Tower of London to mark royal anniversaires and events. They are used also to welcome guests on official State Visits. A special 101-gun salute is fired for coronations at the moment when the crown is placed on the sovereign's head.

The State Opening of Parliament (*photograph page 34*) is an occasion of great pageantry and historic symbolism. The rights of Parliament, established over centuries, are reflected in the ceremony which takes place in the House of Lords. Members of the House of Commons are summoned to hear the "Queen's speech from the throne" formally opening a new session of Parliament.

The Queen travels from Buckingham Palace to Westminster in the Irish State Coach escorted by the Household Cavalry. Another coach conveys the crown and regalia. The route is the traditional processional route - down the Mall, across Horse Guards Parade, through the Horse Guards Arch into Whitehall and on to the House of Lords. Troops line the route and a Guard of Honour awaits the sovereign at the Palace of Westminster.

The royal procession into the chamber is made up of bearers of unique historic titles - such as the Norfolk Herald Extraordinary, Fitzalan Pursuivant Extraordinary, Rouge Dragon Pursuivant, Gold Stick in Waiting or Lady of the Bedchamber. The peers and peeresses of the House of Lords all wear their parliamentary robes; judges of the High Court of Justice sit robed and bewigged before the throne. Black Rod, acting as sovereign's messenger, knocks three times with his rod on the door of the House of Commons summoning the Members of Parliament to hear the Queen's speech.

Each year, a new Lord Mayor of London is elected, and the spectacular ceremony which surrounds his installation reflects the prestige, importance and antiquity of his office. The first Lord Mayor was installed more than 800 years ago.

Above: The Old Bailey.

The Lord Mayor's Show (*photographs pages 36-37*) is an annual pageant surrounding the ceremonial journey he makes on the second Saturday in November to swear an oath of allegiance in front of the Lord Chief Justice. Dressed in his fur-trimmed scarlet gown, a 'Cap of Dignity' and wearing the great five feet long gold chain of office, he first watches a cavalcade of decorated floats pass by his stand at his official residence, the Mansion House. The Lord Mayor then steps into his gilded State Coach and takes up his position of honour at the rear of the procession. Drawn by six matched shire horses, the 18th century coach is guarded by the Lord Mayor's bodyguard, the red-coated and armoured pikemen and musketeers of the Honourable Artillery Company.

The route of the procession to the Royal Courts of Justice in the Strand is via Cheapside and Fleet Street. At the Law Courts, he takes his oath and returns in style to the Mansion House via Victoria Embankment. Two days later, he presides at the splendid Lord Mayor's Inaugural Banquet at the Guildhall, which is traditionally attended by the Prime Minister.

Dressing up in elaborate historic costume is not just a privilege of London's most important citizens. Each year, on the first Sunday in October, a Costermonger's Harvest Festival service is held at St Martins-in-the-Fields at Trafalgar Square. There, London's famous Pearly Kings and Queens can then be seen in their traditional costumes stitched with hundreds of tiny pearl buttons. Even the vicar conducting the service wears a pearly surplice. A costermonger is someone who sells fruit, vegetables or fish in London's streets from a barrow and they dress up in their pearly costumes for charity.

The law is cloaked in tradition and ceremony to reflect its status and dignity. **The Royal Courts of Justice** in the Strand (*photograph page 35*), housed in a collection of Gothic-style buildings begun in 1874, are the central office of the Supreme Court of Judicature for England and Wales. The Central Hall, 238 feet long, 80 feet high and paved with mosaics, is the entrance to the various courts serving the Court of Appeal and the three divisions of Chancery, Queen's Bench and Admiralty and Family. Each year on October 1, a service takes place in Westminster Abbey to mark the opening of the Legal Year. After the services the judges walk in procession across to the House of Lords for the Lord Chancellor's Breakfast (*photograph page 36*).

The four **Inns of Court,** centres for the legal profession, are in the Inner and Middle Temple and Lincoln's Inn and Gray's Inn.

The Temple between the Thames Embankment and Fleet Street in the City is the home of the Inner and Middle Temple (*photograph page 37*). It was originally the headquarters of the Knights Templars, an order of military crusaders of the 12th century. Lawyers have been there since the 14th century. Within the Temple's peaceful precincts is the Temple Church, consisting of a round nave, modelled on the Church of the Holy Sepulchre at Jerusalem and dating from 1185.

The Central Criminal Court (known as the Old Bailey) is the chief court for crimes committed in the Greater London area. On the first two days of each session, the judges carry posies of flowers and sweet herbs are strewn around the courts, a reminder of the days when unpleasant smells wafted from the prison. Newgate Prison stood on the site from the 13th century and was notorious for its conditions until it was pulled down in 1902 when the Central Criminal Court replaced it. The Court is crowned with a copper dome, 195 feet high, which supports the figure of Justice.

North London

The **British Museum** (*photograph page 39*) in Bloomsbury houses the largest and richest collection of the works of man from prehistoric times to the present day.

Founded in 1753, it grew from gifts of collections of manuscripts, papers, books and antiquities including the Royal collections. Money for the original building – £300,000 – was raised by a public lottery in 1755 and the museum opened to the public in 1759. The present building, designed by Sir Robert Smirke, incorporates 44 classical columns in its 370 feet long frontage and took 30 years to complete in the 19th century. Its famous reading room is a huge circular hall covered by a dome 106 feet high and 140 feet across. Famous scholars who researched and studied there include Marx and Lenin.

The British Museum covers a site of more than $11\frac{1}{2}$ acres (4.5 hectares) and houses important displays from Egypt, (the largest collection outside Egypt); Greece, Western Asia, Rome and the East.

Its treasures include Magna Carta, the document which curbed an English king's powers in 1215; William Shakespeare's first folio published in 1623; the Lindisfarne Gospels dating from around 698 AD; the Parthenon sculptures (the Elgin Marbles); the Rosetta Stone which provided the key to deciphering hieroglyphic script unread for 1,400 years; Egyptian mummies including the Thebes mummy, the 12th century Lewis Chessmen; Lewis Carroll's own illustrated version of 'Alice', the Sutton Hoo treasure from the Anglo-Saxon royal ship-burial in Suffolk.

Madame Tussaud's is the home of an equally famous collection – wax effigies of the famous and infamous. Marie Tussaud first began modelling death masks of guillotined victims of the French Revolution. She opened her first exhibition in London in 1835 and the collection moved to its present site in 1884.

Mummy & coffin of a Priestess from Thebes, British Museum.

Right: British Museum.

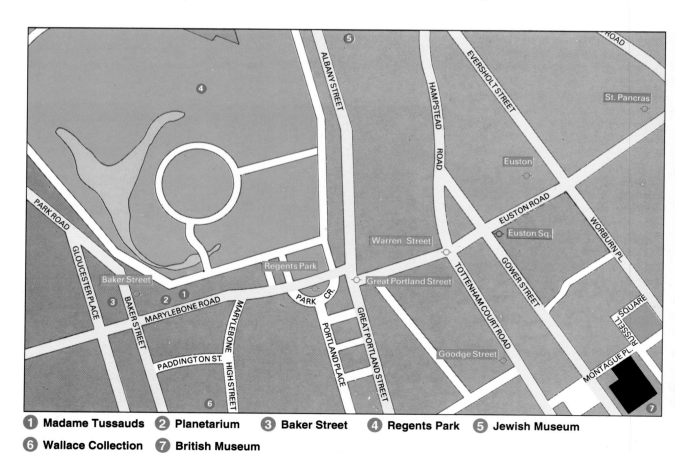

1 Madame Tussauds   **2** Planetarium   **3** Baker Street   **4** Regents Park   **5** Jewish Museum
6 Wallace Collection   **7** British Museum

Horse of Selene from the east pediment of the Parthenon.

Likenesses of world statesmen, the British royal family, sportsmen, writers and artists, film and television stars are featured. To Madame Tussaud's original skill of sculpting in wax has been added the hi-tech refinements of modern electronics and robotics to show pop stars in motion.

In the adjoining **London Planetarium** (*photograph page 40*) opened in 1958 can be seen images of the nigh sky and the planets vividly projected on a multi-dimensional ceiling screen. Man's journeys into space are included in this starshow spectacular.

Baker Street is the fabled home of

Sir Arthur Conan Doyle's famous sleuth Sherlock Holmes. All that can be seen on the site of 221B is the Abbey National Building Society. While Sherlock Holmes was a fictional character, letters are still sent to the address from people all over the world seeking help in solving mysteries of their own.

The **Wallace Collection** of art is set out in Hertford House, an 18th century mansion. It was formerly the home of the Marquesses of Hertford and the collection is a harvest of acquisitions by successive generations of the family.

The collection is notable for its valuable 17th-18th century French paintings, furniture, sculpture and porcelain, European and Oriental arms and armour. Works by English, Dutch, Spanish and Italian artists are included in the treasures.

It was given to the nation in 1897 and opened to the public at the turn of the century.

The Jewish Museum in Albert Street displays ritual objects and antiquities of Jewish life and worship.

Above: The Garden Party at Madame Tussauds.

Right: The Space Trail at The Planetarium.

40

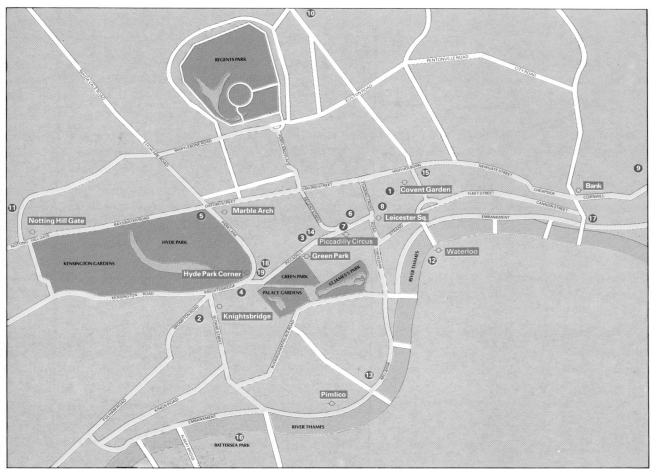

① **Covent Garden** ② **Harrods** ③ **Burlington Arcade** ④ **Hyde Park Corner** ⑤ **Marble Arch** ⑥ **Trocadero**
⑦ **Piccadilly Circus** ⑧ **Leicester Square** ⑨ **Petticoat Lane** ⑩ **Camden Lock** ⑪ **Portobello Road**
⑫ **South Bank Complex** ⑬ **Tate Gallery** ⑭ **Royal Academy** ⑮ **Sir John Soane's Museum**
⑯ **Japanese Pagoda** ⑰ **Monument** ⑱ **Apsley House** ⑲ **Wellington Arch**

Parks

The capital's parks were labelled "the lungs of London" by an 18th century Prime Minister, William Pitt.

The cool, calm and peaceful swathes of green are for London's citizens and visitors a refuge from the roar of a city going about its business. They are also a sanctuary for a wide variety of waterfowl, birds and other wildlife.

London's royal parks were once the private palace playgrounds of princes and monarchs. While they still belong to the Crown today, they are freely open for all to enjoy, though sadly thousands of trees were lost in the storms in Autumn 1987.

Greenwich Park was the first to be fenced and reserved for privileged use in 1433. It was a favourite hunting ground of Tudor monarchs until King Charles II ordered it to be laid out as a park by Le Notre, the landscape gardener of the French king, Louis XIV. The park is still riddled with ancient underground tunnels, probably water conduits for the royal palaces that formerly existed at Greenwich. Flamsteed House, dating from 1675, in the park is the former home of the Royal Observatory. The zero line of longitude passes through the house and is marked by a plate on a path. A visitor can claim to be straddling two halves of the globe by placing a foot at either side of the line. A mast on the turret at Flamsteed House carries a time ball that falls every day a 1pm precisely.

The view from the top of Greenwich Park (*photograph page 42*) takes in Inigo Jones' masterpiece, the Queen's House (now part of the National Maritime Museum), Sir Christopher Wren's Royal Naval College with the river Thames as the backdrop.

Before 1530, **St James's** was marshy land surrounding the leper house of St James. King Henry VIII acquired it for the garden and deer park of his new palace and it is today considered the most beautiful of all the royal parks. Three royal palaces used to border it – Whitehall (burned down in 1698), Westminster and St James's. In King James I's reign, a menagerie existed in the park. A captive elephant is recorded as being given a gallon of wine a day. An aviary was added in the reign of King Charles II, of which

41

the name Birdcage Walk is now the only legacy.

St James's park (*photograph page 43*) was remodelled in 1826 when the architect John Nash created the lake where assorted water fowl now live – including pelicans, originally presented by the Russian ambassador in the 17th century. St James's park fans out to one side of the Victoria Memorial in front of Buckingham Palace. Green Park continues on the other. This is the plainest of London's parks and runs up to **Hyde Park Corner** and the **Wellington Arch** (*photograph page 43*).

The Duke of Wellington, the 'Iron Duke' hero of the Battle of Waterloo lived in the house that faces the busiest traffic island in London. **Apsley House,** (*photograph page 43*) built in 1771-78, is now the Wellington Museum, containing relics of the old soldier. He was a ranger of Hyde Park which forms the backyard to his old home. Letters simply addressed 'Number 1 London' used to reach Wellington at Apsley House.

Hyde Park is 360-acre tract, once part of the manor of Eia owned by Westminster Abbey. It was acquired by King Henry VIII, who traded a priory in Berkshire for it then made it into yet another private royal hunting ground. A century later, King James I and his son Charles I opened it to the public.

Hyde Park is separated from Kensington Gardens by the Serpentine Lake (*photograph page 44*). Together they form the largest open space in central London, a round walk of four miles. Formed by damming the river Westbourne, the Serpentine is the 40-acre habitat of ducks and waterfowl, plus assorted hardy bathers who take a dip every morning of the year, even if it means breaking the ice on its surface.

Hyde Park has been the venue for national celebrations and spectaculars through the ages, from the mass hangings at the Tyburn gallows at its Marble Arch tip to the mock naval battles on the Serpentine in the Georgian era. For King George IV, elephants were towed along the lake on rafts. In 1851 Hyde Park was the setting for the Great Exhibition, a showcase for British skills, goods and crafts under Paxton's glass masterpiece, the

Crystal Palace. The Crystal Palace was taken down after the exhibition and re-erected in south London, but was destroyed by fire in 1936. The money raised by the Great Exhibition funded the national museums (see Kensington section). Duels of honour were traditionally fought in Hyde Park. Modern day, spectaculars include pop concerts and protest meetings.

On the south bank of the River Thames, **Battersea Park** was laid out on a site of Battersea fields where the Duke of Wellington fought a duel with the Earl Winchelsea in 1829. It contains a sub-tropical garden, sculptures by Henry Moore and the striking pagoda (*photograph page 44*) which overlooks the river.

Regent's Park (*photograph page 44*) to the north of London was another happy hunting ground acquired by King Henry VIII. It was remodelled a century and a half ago by John Nash for the Prince Regent who became King George IV. Regent's Park is roughly circular in shape with two lakes and two roads, the Inner Circle and Outer Circle. Ringing the park are graceful terraces of houses. An open air theatre within the Inner Circle stages mainly Shakespearean plays in summer.

Below: Members of the Household Cavalry. pass in front of Wellington Arch.

London Life

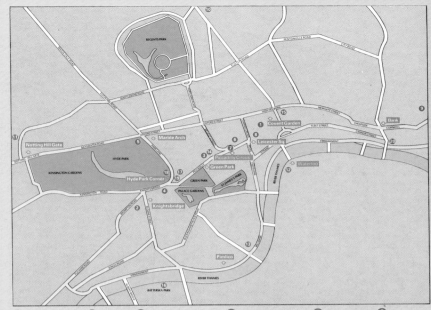

Two hundred years ago, Dr Samuel Johnson wrote: "When a man is tired of London, he is tired of life; for there is in London all that life can afford."

London life offers unrivalled opportunities for entertainment, from its 55 theatres, its cinemas, opera houses, concert hall, casinos, cabaret clubs, nightclubs, wine bars, sports centres and discos. Central London's 1,500 pubs offer a welcome in an infinite variety of ways. Even their names reflect the uniqueness of the English pub character, from the Frog and Nightgown, to The Queen's Head and Artichoke to the more bizarre I Am The Only Running Footman.

Covent Garden is a newly polished jewel on the entertainment scene, although its origins date back centuries. It was the "convent

① Covent Garden ② Harrods ③ Burlington Arcade ④ Hyde Park Corner ⑤ Marble Arch ⑥ Trocadero ⑦ Piccadilly Circus ⑧ Leicester Square ⑨ Petticoat Lane ⑩ Camden Lock ⑪ Portobello Road ⑫ South Bank Complex ⑬ Tate Gallery ⑭ Royal Academy · ⑮ Sir John Soane's Museum ⑯ Japanese Pagoda ⑰ Monument ⑱ Apsley House ⑲ Wellington Arch

garden" of the monks of Westminster Abbey and was laid out as a select residential area by Inigo Jones in the 17th century, complete with a small market. A building housing London's fruit and vegetable market was constructed in 1833, and this, restored and transformed in 1980, is the focal point of the Covent Garden area (*photograph page 45*). It is now a pedestrian precinct bristling with specialist shops, craft stalls, cafes, bars and buskers. These colourful street entertainers (*photograph page 46*) perform in the piazza or square which separates the old market building from St Paul's Church, known as the actor's church. The range of free entertainment is vast – from one-man renditions of Shakespeare to robotic dancing to disco music; from comic mime to classical music. The imposing columned portico of St Paul's forms the backdrop to their acts. This scene formed the setting for the start of Shaw's play Pygmalion (My Fair Lady).

Literary lions of the 17th and 18th century – Dryden, Pope, Swift, Fielding and Johnson – used to frequent the coffee houses of Russell Street in the Covent Garden area. The Royal Opera House, known as the Coven Garden Theatre, is the principal home of ballet and opera in London and the old flower market to the south-east of the square now houses two museums: the London Transport museum where predecessors of the distinctive red London bus are on display, and the Theatre Museum which is a major centre for students of the performing arts.

Piccadilly Circus (*photograph page 47*) has become an important meeting point – for traffic as well as sightseers. At its heart is a bronze fountain topped by a figure of a winged archer, popularly known as Eros, the pagan god of love, but designed as a memorial to Lord Shaftesbury, a 19th century philanthropist and intended to represent Christian charity. The name Piccadilly stems from a 17th century dressmaker who lived in the area and created a frilled collar called a 'piccadil'.

The **Trocadero Centre** nearby is a shopping and restaurant complex with high-tech entertainment, a large cinema complex and an exhibition bringing to life the events, achievements and oddities featured in the Guinness Book of Records.

In 1989 the refurbished London Pavillion opened. One floor is devoted to a new and exciting Madame Tussaud's exhibition: Rock Circus (*photograph page 47*).

Leciester Square comes to life at night, when cinema fans throng the square which is surrounded by large cinema complexes. The square was laid out in the 17th century and named after the Earl of Leicester,

who lived nearby. The painters Hogarth and Reynolds were also famous residents.

Gentlemen used to fight duels of honour in the square, but it was converted in 1874 into a public garden and now features statues of two giants of the entertainment industry – William Shakespeare and Charlie Chaplin.

The cosmopolitan, brash and bustling area of Soho comes alive at

night as the adult centre of London. It boasts an infinite variety of restaurants and theatres, clubs and bars.

London is a shoppers' paradise. Its best known store is **Harrods** (*photograph page 48*) in Knightsbridge, a red terracotta building whose interior decoration includes Art Nouveau and Art Deco styles. With a staff of around 5,000, its proud boast is that it can supply anything to anyone

anywhere and it has obliged by delivering an elephant to Ronald Reagan, gooseberries to Saudi Arabia and a skunk to an American's ex-wife. Harrods was the first store in the world to install an escalator, and Victorian customers were so overcome by the experience of riding a "moving staircase" that the store posted attendants at the top to administer brandy to gentlemen and smelling salts to the ladies.

Oxford Street is lined with large department stores including Selfridges, John Lewis and Marks and Spencer. It runs the route of an old Roman road called the Via Trinovantino which crossed another important Roman road at Marble Arch.

A smaller and more exclusive shopping promenade can be found in Piccadilly. **The Burlington Arcade** (*photograph page 48*) is a forerunner of the modern shopping mall. This privately owned arcade, built in 1819 and 585 feet long, contains 72 shops. It retains its Regency character: uniformed Beadles are on duty to ensure that everyone obeys the rules, which includes a ban on whistling and opening umbrellas. A plaque on the wall declares that it was opened by the Duchess of Devonshire together with a London dustman.

Democracy gives a free and entertaining display at Hyde Park's **Speaker's Corner**. Anyone can address the people and put forward their views no matter how outrageous or crackpot. *(photograph page 49)*

London's markets provide a happy hunting ground for dedicated bargain spotters. **Petticoat Lane** in the East End of London is open on Sundays and, in the words of a song written about it, can supply anything, from "a ball of string, a second-hand chinchilla or a diamond ring". The **Caledonian**, **Portobello Road** *(photographs pages 49)* and **Greenwich markets** feature antiques. **Camden Lock**, on a canal setting to the north of London, is a colourful jumble of bric-a-brac, crafts, old clothes and quirky up-to-the-minute fashions.

Up-market entertainment is provided at the **South Bank** complex, *(photograph page 50)* the world's largest centre for arts. The Royal Festival, Queen Elizabeth and Purcell Room concert halls, together with the National Theatre, the National Film Theatre and the Hayward

49

Gallery which form the South Bank complex are a permanent souvenir of the Festival of Britain in 1951, a tonic for the nation after the deprivations of the Second World War.

On the north bank of the Thames at Millbank is the **Tate Gallery**. Sugar magnate Sir Henry Tate commissioned the classical fronted building and it opened in 1897 to display a significant part of the national collection of British painting, including his own collection of more than 60 works. The Tate is renowned for its modern works of art.

The **Royal Academy** in Piccadilly encourages excellence in British art and its Summer Exhibitions display the work of talented living artists.

Sir John Soane's Museum at Lincoln's Inn Fields is a collection of the works of art and furniture the noted architect gathered over his lifetime. On his death in 1837 he left his home and its contents for the nation to enjoy, and the collection can be viewed today much as Sir John himself arranged it.

River Thames

The **River Thames** (*photograph page 51*) threads its way through the capital, linking London to a string of strategic and historic sites on its 210 mile journey from its source to the sea.

The river has been used continuously as a highway since prehistoric times. The Romans built the first bridge across it and laid the foundations for the city they called Londinium, although the name London probably arose from the Celtic words Llyn-din meaning river place.

The first stone-built London Bridge spanned the riverbanks eight hundred years ago. It was the capital's only bridge across the Thames until 1749. There are now 28 bridges (including railway bridges) between Teddington and Tower Bridge.

Londoners used their river for more than just a thoroughfare. During the 17th and 18th centuries, Frost Fairs were held on its frozen water. Stalls, performing artists — even a performing bear and an ox roast on the ice — entertained visitors.

Yet the river which gave London life also brought death. It was used as a sewer, and its waters were so foul by Victorian times that cholera was a major hazard. Official committees were set up to find ways of curing the capital's unhealthy 'Big Stink' of 1858. Curtains soaked in chloride of lime were hung at the windows of the House of Commons and plans were drawn up to move Parliament and the Law Courts out of London where the air was fresher.

An engineer, Sir Joseph Bazalgette, was employed to solve the problem. He began in 1864 by building the **Embankment** along the riverbank. His scheme reclaimed 37 acres of mud flats for a road and ornamental gardens. Underneath the Embankment runs the main sewer which cured London's sanitary problems. It is high enough in places to accommodate a red double decker bus.

The River Thames is now probably the cleanest metropolitan river in the world. Twelve million people depend on it for their domestic water supply and more than 100 different varieties of fish live in it.

Westminster Bridge is a central point from which London can be explored by river. Wordsworth thought nothing on earth was more fair than the view from Westminster Bridge. Queen Boadicea's statue (*photograph page 52*) is near the spot where the Romans probably first crossed the Thames. Pleasure craft ply downstream to The Tower, Greenwich and the Thames Barrier and upstream to Kew and Hampton Court. Windsor Castle lies further on up the river.

The river landscape has evolved over the centuries. Redevelopment is now breathing new life into London's once teeming but now redundant dock areas totalling 8½ square miles along the riverbanks. Springing up in the once derelict docklands are 'mini Venices' — offices, shopping and watersport facilities, homes, heritage trails, factories, a light railway and even an airport. **St Katharine's dock** (*photograph page 53*) by the Tower is now a yacht harbour. On the riverside promenade is the modern bronze fountain sculpture 'Girl with a Dolphin.'

HMS Belfast, an 11,500 ton cruiser which opened the bombardment of the Normandy coast on D-Day is just one of the historic ships moored on the Thames' banks. HMS Belfast is a floating museum opposite the Tower of London. Three ships, Wellington, Chrysanthemum and President, are permanently moored along the Embankment. The Wellington is the floating headquarters of a City livery company while the others are training ships.

Britain was for centuries a great sea-power, and **Greenwich**, five miles downstream from London Bridge, represents the maritime might of the nation. Four-square on the river bank is one of Sir Christopher Wren's masterpieces, the Royal Naval College (*photograph page 54*) built around the turn of the 18th century on the site of a royal palace, the Placentia. The buildings, consisting of four separate blocks, feature the Painted Hall with ceiling paintings by Sir James Thornhill and the Chapel with a 25 feet high altarpiece painting by Benjamin West of St Paul shaking off the Viper.

Behind it and part of the impressive view from the river is the National Maritime Museum, containing records and relics of 500 years of naval history. It is partly based in the Queen's House, designed by Inigo Jones in 1616 as a palace for King James I's consort Anne of Denmark. It is considered one of the finest Renaissance buildings in the country. A graceful colonnade links the west and east wings built in the early 19th century.

The Cutty Sark, (*photograph page*

56)a Victorian sailing clipper, rests in dry dock on the river bank at Greenwich and nearby is Sir Francis Chichester's yacht, Gipsy Moth IV in which he sailed single-handed around the world in 1966-67.

The Thames Barrier (*photograph page 56*) at Woolwich Reach is a modern miracle of engineering which guards 45 square miles of the vulnerable heart of London from flooding. Fourteen people died 60 years ago when Central London was flooded. Yet the high tide levels in London are rising and the Thames Barrier is part of the capital's defences. Conceived on a scale unequalled anywhere in the world, it consists of 10 separate pivoting steel gates strung out in a 1,689 feet line across the river. Four main gates each heavier than a naval destroyer stand as high as a 5-storey building. Shipping can pass between the gates, but when storm and tide warnings are posted, the protective barrier can swing into place within 30 minutes to block the threatening water from surging up the Thames. It was first used to counter potential danger in February 1983.

Upstream from Westminster lies Kew and the **Royal Botanic Gardens**, one of the most famous collections of plants and flowers in the world. Thirty thousand varieties of plants and trees grow on the 300-acre site including tropical and water species.

The Princess of Wales conservatory features lilies six feet wide (*photograph page 56*). A further seven million dried specimens are preserved in the Herbarium. Unfortunately during the autumn of 1987 the gardens sustained serious storm damage and lost many of their trees.

Kew was the inspiration of Princess Augusta, mother of King George III, who began the garden as a hobby in 1759. As the project literally blossomed, she commissioned temples and the 10-storey pagoda (*photograph page 57*) to add interest among the greenery. Kew was presented to the nation to enjoy in 1841 yet its most important role now is as a scientific institution.

Further on up the Thames is **Hampton Court Palace,** *(photographs pages 58/59)* the grandest house of all in 16th century England. Cardinal Wolsey, one of the most powerful political figures of the time, ordered it tobe built with no expense spared. Its 1,000 rooms were not only sumptuous; they enjoyed the latest sanitary technology. Wolsey was just as keen on drains as decor and 250 tons of lead were used to build a three and a half mile pipline to bring clean spring water to Hampton Court. King Henry VIII's royal barge was just one of the many bringing impressive visitors via the Thames to enjoy the lavish lifestyle at Hampton Court.

But Wolsey had little time to enjoy it before an increasingly irritated King Henry VIII siezed Hampton Court and its land for himself and imprisoned the Cardinal.

Hampton Court became a royal

playground for the king and his numerous queens. Henry continued to pour vast sums of money into the grand house. He rebuilt the Great Hall, completed the chapel and created new royal lodgings, indoor and outdoor tennis courts, three bowling alleys and tiltyard for jousting. The Astronomical Clock in Clock Court tells not only the hour, but also the day, month and the phases of the moon. It also shows the sun revolving round the earth, as it was built before the great astronomers understood the mysteries of our solar system.

Hampton Court became a favourite royal palace for successive monarchs. Architect Sir Christopher Wren modernised and remodeled Hampton Court in the following century.

The State rooms have been open to the public since 1838, soon after young Victoria came to the throne.

Its gardens contain the maze commissioned by King William in the 17th century after the death of his wife Mary.

Windsor Castle (*photograph page 61*) continues the link with London via the Thames. Its name probably derives from Windleshore, a reference to the many bends in the river at this point. Windsor's strategic site high above the Thames led to it being chosen by William the Conqueror for his castle – part of a chain of fortresses with which he planned to encircle London. Building started in 1070 and it has been used since then as a royal home for over 900 years.

Henry II (1154-89) built the distinctive Round Tower and outer walls. Its defences have been attacked only twice in nine centuries – in 1193 when Richard I was away on a crusade and later when barons rose up against King John's power. This led to a historic document called Magna Carta in 1215 which protected an individual's personal and political liberty.

Edward III turned Windsor into a more comfortable royal residence in the 14th century and kings and queens through the ages have left their mark.

St George's Chapel, the chapel of the Knights of the Garter, is a masterpiece of Perpendicular Gothic architecture. Dedicated to thepatron saint of England, it rivals Westminster Abbey as the most hallowed shrine for British monarchy through the ages. It is the chapel of the Knights of the Garter, an exclusive chivalrous order which meets at Windsor for the Garter service, one of the most colourful and important ceremonies in the royal calendar. The Order is popularly thought to have originated in 1348 when King Edward II danced at a ball at Windsor with Joanne, Countess of Salisbury. The noble lady's blue garter fell off. Edward is reputed to have stooped to scoop it up and to silence the titters of the other dancers, he vowed that in a short time they would see the garter 'advanced to so high honour and estimation as to account themselves happy to wear it.' The sovereign appoints her 24 Knights Companion.

The reign of King George IV in the 19th century saw the fortress at Windsor turned into a sumptuous royal palace. The State Apartments, which include the Grand Reception Room, the Waterloo Chamber, the Garter Throne Room and St George's Hall display fine carvings, furniture, tapestries and paintings.

The treasures of Windsor Castle include Queen Mary's Dolls' House. It was designed by the great architect Sir Edwin Lutyens to reflect life in a royal palace in the early part of this century. Every feature is to the scale of one inch to one foot and the dolls'

Photographs on pages 58 and 59 are of Hampton Court Palace. Top left is of the main entrance, bottom left is the view from the east. Above is the Clock Court.

house is in full working order even down to the light bulbs the size of teardrops and the kitchen's hot and cold running water.

Windsor Great Park covering 4,800 acres was a traditional royal hunting ground. It is connected to the castle by a straight drive three miles long called Long Walk. Laid out in 1685 to provide an unrivalled view from the castle, it features an equestrian statue of King George III.

When the Queen is in residence at Windsor, the Royal Standard is flown from the Round Tower.

The purpose of this guidebook has been to provide a pictorial shop-window of the rich, historic and varied pleasures London has to offer. For those visitors who have already sampled some of the delights of London for themselves, it is our hope that this colourful souvenir will preserve your memories and remind you to come back again soon.

The Queen's Ball Room.
A State Visit at Windsor Castle.

Details of major centres of interest.

Key:

 Nearest London Transport Underground Station.

 Nearest British Rail Station.

Most places of interest are closed on Christmas Day, Boxing Day, New Years Day, Good Friday and May Bank Holiday. Please check details at these times.

Albert Memorial
Kensington Gore, SW7
South Kensington/High St. Kensington

Alien War
Trocadero Centre, Coventry Street, W1
Tel: 0171 437 2678
Open: Mon-Fri 1130-2300 Sat 1030-2300
Piccadilly Circus

Apsley House
149 Piccadilly, W1 Tel: 0171-499 5676
Open: Tues -Sun 1100-1700
Hyde Park Corner

Bank of England Museum
Bartholomew Lane, EC2 Tel: 0171-601 5545
Open: Mon-Fri 1000-1700 (from Good Friday to end Sept also open Sun & Bank Holidays 1100-1700)
Bank (Liverpool Street, Fenchurch Street, Cannon Street weekdays only)

Banqueting House
Whitehall, SW1 Tel: 0171-839 8919
Open: Mon-Sat 1000-1700. May be closed at short notice for Government functions.
Westminster

British Museum
Great Russell St., WC1 Tel: 0171-636 1555
Open: Mon to Sat 1000-1700.
Sun 1430-1800.
Tottenham Court Rd./Russell Square

Buckingham Palace
SW1 Tel: 0171-839 1377
Open: Aug & Sep, daily 0930-1730; ticket office opens at 0900 and closes when the last ticket has been sold. Visitors are advised to buy their tickets before midday.
St. James's Park/Green Park/Victoria

Cabinet War Rooms
Clive Steps, King Charles St., SW1
Tel: 0171-930 6961
Open: 1 Apr-30 Sept, daily 0930-1800; 1 Oct-31 Mar, daily 1000-1800 (last admission 1715)
Westminster

Camden Lock Market
NW1
Open: Sat & Sun 0900-1800
Camden Town/Chalk Farm

Changing Guard Ceremonies
Buckingham Palace - April to end of July daily, at 1130 (alternate days from August to end of March). To avoid disappointment call 0839 123411
St. James's Park/Green Park/Victoria

Horse Guards, Whitehall - Daily Mon to Sat at 1100, 1000 on Sundays.
To avoid disappointment call 0839 123411
Westminster/Charing Cross

Commonwealth Institute
Kensington High St., W8 Tel: 0171-603 4535
Open: Mon to Sat 1000-1700 Sun 1400-1700
High Street Kensington

Cutty Sark (Clipper ship)
King William Walk, Greenwich, SE10 Tel: 0181-858 3445
Open: Oct to March, Mon to Sat 1000-1700, Sun 1200-1700.
April to Sept, Mon to Sat 1000-1800, Sun 1200-1800
Greenwich or Maze Hill or boat from Westminster, Charing Cross or Tower Pier to Greenwich Pier.

Dickens House
48 Doughty Street, WC1 Tel: 0171-405 2127
Open: Mon-Sat 1000-1700. Closed Sun and selected days at Christmas.
Russell Square/Chancery Lane

Gipsy Moth IV
Cutty Sark Gardens, Greenwich, SE10 Tel: 0181-858 3445
Open: April to Oct Mon to Sat 1000-1300 & 1400-1730, Sun 1200-1730
Same as Cutty Sark

Guards Museum
Birdcage Walk, SW1 Tel: 0171-414 3271
Open: Daily (except Friday's) 1000-1600
St. James's Park

Guildhall
Gresham St., EC2 Tel: 0171-606 3030
Open: Mon to Sat 1000-1700, Sun (May-Sept) & Spring/Autumn Bank Holiday 1000-1700
Bank/St. Paul's/Mansion House

Guinness World of Records
The Trocadero Centre
Piccadilly Circus, W1 Tel: 0171-439 7331
Open: Daily 1000-2200
Piccadilly Circus/Leicester Square

Hampton Court Palace
East Molesey, Surrey Tel: 0181-781 9500
Open: Mid Mar-Mid Oct, Mon 1015-1800,
Tues-Sun 0930-1800; Mid Oct-Mid Mar Mon 1015-1630,
Tues-Sun 0930-1630
Hampton Court

Hayward Gallery
South Bank, Belvedere Rd., SE1 Tel: 0171-261 0127
Open: Mon-Wed 1000-2000, Thurs-Sat 1000-1800, Sun 1200-1800
Closed between exhibitions
Waterloo

HMS Belfast
Morgan's Lane, Tooley St, SE1 Tel: 0171-407 6434
Open: Daily, Summer 1000-1800, Winter 1000-1700
London Bridge. Ferry from Tower Pier

Houses of Parliament
Parliament Square, SW1 Tel: 0171-219 3090/3100
Open: (to watch debate) - House of Commons, Mon to Thurs from 1615, Fri from 1000, to Strangers' gallery.

House of Lords, Tues, Wed, Thurs and some Mons, admission from 1430
Westminster

Imperial War Museum
Lambeth Road, SE1 Tel: 0171-416 5000
Open: Daily 1000-1800.
Lambeth North/Elephant & Castle

Jewish Museum
Raymond Burton House, 129 Albert St, NW1
Tel: 0171-284 1997
Open: Sun-Thu 1000-1600. Closed Jewish festivals and public holidays
Camden Town

Kensington Palace State Apartments
Kensington Gardens, W8 Tel: 0171-937 9561
Open: Mon to Sat 0900-1700, Sun 1100-1700
Due to close for refurbishment in Autumn 1995 for approx 18 months
Queensway/Kensington High St

Kew Gardens (Royal Botanic Gardens)
Kew, Richmond, Surrey Tel: 0181-940 1171
Open: Daily from 0930 - please call for closing times
Kew Gardens

London Brass Rubbing Centre
St Martin-in-the-Fields Church, Trafalgar Square, WC2
Tel: 0171 437 6023
Open: Mon-Sat 1000-1800, Sun 1200-1800.
Charing Cross

London Dungeon
28/34 Tooley Street, SE1 Tel: 0171-403 0606
Open: Daily April-Sept: 1000-1730, Oct-March 1000-1630
London Bridge

London Planetarium
Marylebone Rd., NW1 Tel: 0171-486 1121
Open: During termtime - Star shows last 30 minutes and are at Mon-Fri 1220 and every 40 minutes until 1600 (last show), Sat-Sun from 1020 until 1700. During school holidays 1020-1700
Baker Street

London Toy and Model Museum
21-23 Craven Hill, W2 Tel: 0171-706 8000
Open: Daily 1000-1730, Sun 1100-1730
Lancaster Gate/Bayswater/Queensway

London Transport Museum
Covent Garden, WC2 Tel: 0171-379 6344
Open: Daily 1000-1800
Covent Garden/Leicester Square

London Zoo
Regents Park, NW1 Tel: 0171-722 3333
Open: Daily Mar-Sept 1000-1730, Oct-Feb 1000-1600
Camden Town

Madame Tussaud's
Marylebone Rd., NW1 Tel: 0171-935 6861
Open: Mon-Fri 1000-1730, Sat, Sun 0930-1730
Baker St.

Museum of London
London Wall, EC2 Tel: 0171-600 3699
Open: Tues to Sat 1000-1750, Sun 1400-1750
St. Paul's/Barbican/Moorgate

Museum of Mankind
6 Burlington Gardens, W1 Tel: 0171-323 8043
Open: Mon to Sat 1000-1700, Sun 1430-1800
Piccadilly Circus/Green Park

Museum of the Moving Image
South Bank, Waterloo, SE1 Tel: 0171-928 3535
Open: Daily 1000-1800
Waterloo/Embankment

National Army Museum
Royal Hospital Road, SW3 Tel: 0171-730 0717
Open: Daily 1000-1730
Sloane Square then 10-15 minutes walk

National Gallery
Trafalgar Square, WC2 Tel: 0171-839 3321
Open: Mon to Sat 1000-1800, Sun 1400-1800
Charing Cross/Leicester Square

National Maritime Museum
Romney Rd., Greenwich, SE10 Tel: 0181-858 4422
Open: Mon to Sat 1000-1700, Sun 1200-1800 (Summer).
Sun 1400-1700 (Winter)
Maze Hill or boat from Westminster, Charing Cross
and Tower Pier to Greenwich Pier.

National Portrait Gallery
St. Martins Place, WC2 Tel: 0171-306 0055
Open: Mon to Sat 1000-1800, Sun 1200-1800
Charing Cross/Leicester Square

Natural History Museum
Cromwell Rd., South Kensington, SW7 Tel: 0171-938 9123
Open: Mon to Sat 1000-1750, Sun 1100-1750
South Kensington

Old Royal Observatory
Greenwich Park, SE10 Tel: 0181-858 4422
Open: Apr-Sep, Mon-Sat 1000-1700, Sun 1200-1700; Oct-
Mar, Mon-Sat 1000-1700, Sun 1400-1700
Maze Hill, Boat from Westminster, Charing Cross,
Tower Pier to Greenwich Pier

Petticoat Lane Market
Middlesex St., E1
Main market open Sun 0900-1400
Aldgate East/Liverpool St.

Portobello Rd Market, W11
Open: Mon to Thurs 0900-1600 (approx.), Fri & Sat 0800-
1700 (approx.) (Antiques Sat only)
Ladbroke Grove/Notting Hill Gate

Queen's Gallery
Buckingham Palace Rd., SW1 Tel: 0171-839 1377
Open: Daily 0930-1630. Closed between exhibitions.
Victoria/St. James's Park

Rock Circus
London Pavillion, No. 1 Piccadilly, W1 Tel: 0171-734 7203
Open: Mon-Thu 1100-2100, Fri & Sat 1100-2200, Sun
1100-2100. During Easter and summer holidays 1000-2200.
Piccadilly Circus

Royal Academy of Arts
Burlington House, Piccadilly, W1 Tel: 0171-439 7438
Open: Daily 1000-1800
Piccadilly Circus/Green Park

Royal Albert Hall
Kensington Gore, SW7 Tel: 0171-589 8212
Open: (box office) Mon to Sat 1000-1800, Sun 1000-1800
(approx.)
South Kensington/High Street Kensington

Royal Courts of Justice
Strand, WC2 Tel: 0171-936 6000
Open: Mon to Fri 0900-1700
Temple/Chancery Lane

Royal Mews
Buckingham Palace Rd., SW1 Tel: 0171-839 1377
Open: Jan to Mid March Wed 1200-1600; Mid March to beg
Aug Tues-Thurs 1200-1600; beg Aug to Sept Mon-Thurs
1200-1600; Oct to Dec Wed 1200-1600
Victoria

St. Paul's Cathedral
Ludgate Hill, EC4 Tel: 0171-248 2705
Open: For worship - Mon-Sat 0715-1800, Sun 0745-1700;
Cathedral sightseeing Mon-Sat 0830-1600; Crypt and Ambulatory
open 0845-1615; Galleries Mon-Sat 1000-1615. Special services or
events may close some or all parts of the cathedral
St. Paul's/Mansion House

Science Museum
Exhibition Rd., SW7 Tel: 0171-938 8000
Open: Mon to Sat 1000-1800, Sun 1100-1800
South Kensington

Shakespeare Globe Theatre and Exhibition
New Globe Walk, Bankside, SE1 Tel: 0171-928 6406
Open: Daily 1000-1700.
London Bridge/Mansion House
London Bridge

Sir John Soane's Museum
13 Lincoln's Inn Fields, WC2 Tel: 0171-405 2107
Open: Tues to Sat 1000-1700 first Tues in month 1800-2100
Holborn

Tate Gallery
Millbank, SW1 Tel: 0171-887 8000
Open: Mon to Sat 1000-1750, Sun 1400-1750
Pimlico

Thames Barrier Visitors Centre
Unity Way, Woolwich, SE18 Tel: 0181-854 1373
Open: Mon to Fri 1000-1700, Sat & Sun 1030-1730
Charlton. Boat from Westminster Pier or via
Greenwich

Tower Bridge
SE1 Tel: 0171-403 3761
Open: 1st April to 31st Oct 1000-1830, last entry 1745. 1st
Nov to 31st March 1000-1715, last entry 1600
Tower Hill

Tower Hill Pageant
Tower Hill, EC3 Tel: 0171-709 0081
Open: 1st April to 31st Oct 0930-1730, 1st Nov to 31st Mar
0930-1630
Tower Hill

Tower of London
Tower Hill, EC3 Tel: 0171-709 0765
Open: Mar to Oct, Mon to Sat 0900-1800. Sun 1000-1800
Nov to Feb, Mon to Sat 0900-1700 Sun 1000-1700
Tower Hill

Trooping the Colour
From Buckingham Palace, SW1 along the Mall to Horse
Guards Parade, Whitehall and back again. Time: The
Queen's official birthday (2nd Sat in June) at 1100
Charing Cross/Westminster

Victoria & Albert Museum
Cromwell Rd., SW7 Tel: 0171-938 8500
Open: Tues to Sun 1000-1750, Mon 1200-1750
South Kensington

Wallace Collection
Hertford House, Manchester Square, W1 Tel: 0171-935 0687
Open: Mon to Sat 1000-1700 Sun 1400-1700
Bond St.

Wembley Stadium Tours
Wembley, Middlesex Tel: 0181-902 8833
Open: Apr-Sep, daily tours from 1000-1600, Oct-Mar, daily
tours from 1000-1500. No tours on Event days.
Wembley Park

Westminster Abbey
Parliament Square, SW1 Tel: 0171-222 5152
Open: Mon to Sun Nave & Cloisters 0800-1800, Chapels,
Mon-Fri 0920-1600, Sat 0920-1445, 1600-1800
Westminster/St. Jameses' Park

Westminster Cathedral
Ashley Place, SW1 Tel: 0171-834 7452
Open: Daily 0700-2000, Christmas Day 0700-1630
Victoria/St. James's Park

Windsor Castle
Windsor, Berkshire Tel: (01753) 831118
Open: Throughout the year. For full details please phone.

These places of interest are also accessable by bus. For
information and free bus maps please call:
London Transport, 55 Broadway, London SW1
Tel: 0171-222 1234 (24 hour service, 7 days a week)

The main tourist information centres are located at:
London Tourist Board Information Centre
Victoria Station Forecourt, SW1
Centre open daily 0800-1800

City of London Information Centre
St. Paul's Churchyard, EC4 Tel: 0171-606 3030
Open: April to Sept, Mon to Sat 1000-1600
Oct to March, 1000-1430, closed 1300-1400

British Travel Centre
12 Regent St., Piccadilly Circus, SW1
Open: Mon to Fri 0900-1830, Winter Sat & Sun 1000-1600
Summer Sat & Sun 0900-1700

*Although every care has been taken in producing accurate
information for this list, the publishers cannot accept responsibility
for any error or omissions.*

KEY TO MAP

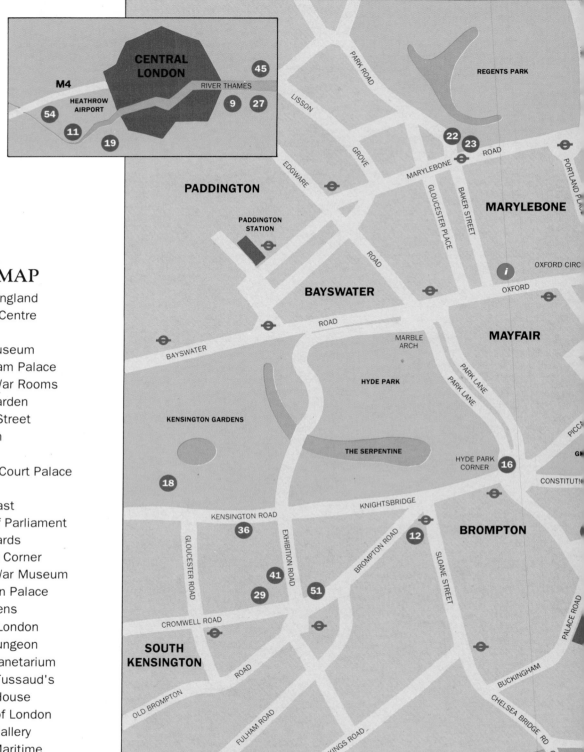